365 DAYS
of Kingdom

Blessings
Volume 1

Scriptures taken from Holy Bible,
New Living Translation, NLT®.
Copyright © 1996, 2004, 2015 by
Tyndale House Foundation. Used by
permission of Tyndale House
Publishers, Inc., Carol Stream,
Illinois 60188. All rights reserved.

Published by:
EMPOWER ME BOOKS, I.N.C.
A Subsidiary of
Empower Me Enterprises, Inc.
P.O. Box 16153
Durham, North Carolina 27704
www.EmpowerMeBooks.com

ISBN: 978-1954418905
Printed in The United States of America

Winter Spring

Faith Hope Love Advancement

Forward Movement

Faith

John 1:1 (KJV)

*In the beginning was the
Word, and the Word was
with God, and the Word
was God.*

Let the word of God
be your source for
every situation.

Faith

Psalm 118:24 (KJV)

This is the day the LORD has made. We will rejoice and be glad in it.

Let the breaking of day bring fullness of joy. Because true joy is never dependent on your circumstances.

Day
3

Faith

**Nehemiah 8:10
(KJV)**

*The joy of the Lord is my
strength.*

Joy from His strength
breeds inner peace to
overcome any
adversity.

Faith

Psalm 91:1 (KJV)

*He that dwelleth in the
secret place of the Most
High shall abide under
the shadow of the
Almighty.*

Abiding under the
shadow of God's
wings means that you
choose to live a life
under the divine
protection of the
Most Highest God.

Faith

John 3:16 (KJV)

For God so loved the world that he gave his one and only Son, that whoever believes in him shall not perish but have eternal life.

Because of the love of God, the Father, He saw the need of His creation known as mankind. Do not let sin cause you to choose darkness over the Light.

Faith

John 14:1 (KJV)

Let not your heart be troubled: ye believe in God, believe also in me.

Do not lose all hope in what you experience in this world, because we have hope through the Lord Jesus Christ.

Psalm 107:20 (KJV)

*He sent his word, and
healed them, and
delivered them from their
destructions.*

Christ who is the
Word is the essential
cure. Let the Word of
God heal you from
guilt, bad habits,
depression, and any
manner of sickness
and sin.

Faith

John 1:14 (KJV)

The Word became flesh and made his dwelling among us. We have seen his glory, the glory of the one and only Son, who came from the Father, full of grace and truth.

Put your trust and confidence in the Word of God. It contains everything you need.

Day

9

Faith

Philippians 4:19
(KJV)

*But my God shall supply
all your need according to
his riches in glory by
Christ Jesus.*

The Lord promises to
meet every need you
have. Do not put
your faith in the
circumstance.

Day
10

Faith

Psalm 23:1 (KJV)

The LORD is my shepherd; I shall not want.

The Lord is the good Shepherd; Therefore, there is nothing the Lord would not do for you that is within His will. It is His good pleasure to take care of you.

Faith

John 4:24 (NIV)

God is a Spirit, and his worshipers must worship in the Spirit and in truth.

Worship God with a sincere heart, not only in praise and thanksgiving but also by your words and deeds.

Day

12

Faith

Hebrews 11:1(KJV)

Now faith is the substance of things hoped for, the evidence of things not seen.

Faith is holding to God's word, with an understanding that faith is the substance of what the word promises. Hold on to your faith and do not let it go. Even when you cannot see what you are believing God for.

Faith

Exodus 34:10 (KJV)

And he said, Behold, I make a covenant: before all your people I will do marvels, such as have not been done in all the earth, nor in any nation: and all the people among which you are shall see the work of the LORD: for it is a terrible thing that I will do with you.

God has established a new covenant. He will continue to do awesome things in your life. Rejoice in knowing that because of his love, greatness is in you.

Faith

Jeremiah 29:11 (KJV)

For I know the thoughts that I think toward you, said the LORD, thoughts of peace, and not of evil, to give you an expected end.

Take time today to renew your mind to what God has to say about your life and success in your health, relationships, and

finances.

Faith

Matthew
17:20 (ESV)

He said to them, Because of your little faith. For truly, I say to you, if you have faith like a grain of mustard seed, you will say to this mountain, move from here to there, and it will move, and

nothing will be impossible for you.

The seed of your faith will help you overcome the mountains you may face in life.

Faith

Romans 1:17 (ESV)

*For in it the righteousness
of God is revealed from
faith for faith, as it is
written, the righteous
shall live by faith.*

Let your faith work
for you. Faith will
take you to higher
heights and deeper
depths.

Faith

James 2:17 (KJV)

Even so faith, if it hath not works, is dead, being alone.

Do not let the lack of the works of your faith cause you to fall into dead situations.

Faith

Ephesians 6:16 (KJV)

Above all, taking the shield of faith, wherewith ye shall be able to quench all the fiery darts of the wicked.

True faith manifests itself through your actions.

Faith

James 2:24 (NIV)

You see that a person is considered righteous by what they do and not by faith alone.

It is when you move in faith that you will be able to overcome. You are justified through Christ by your faith.

Faith

**II Corinthians 5:7
(KJV)**

*For we walk by faith, not
by sight.*

Do not be blinded by
watered-down faith in
what you cannot
physically see.

Faith

Proverbs 3:5 (KJV)

Trust in the LORD with all thine heart; and lean not unto thine own understanding.

Completely trust God, because He alone is Omniscient, the only one who knows all things.

Faith

Isaiah 55:8 (NLT)

*My thoughts are nothing like
your thoughts, says the LORD.
And my ways are far beyond
anything you could
imagine.*

The things that God
thinks and purposes
are not the things that
we think and purpose.
We must begin to
think with the mind
of God because the
thoughts of God are
different.

Faith

Luke 17:5-6 (KJV)

*And the apostles said
unto the Lord, Increase our faith.
And the Lord said, if ye had
faith as a grain of mustard seed,
ye might say unto this
sycamine tree, be thou plucked up
by the root, and be thou planted
in the sea; and it should obey you.*

The size of your faith
matters. Because faith
is what pleases God.

Faith

Mark 9:23 (ESV)

And Jesus said to him, "If you can'! All things are possible for one who believes."

Can God? Yes, God can. If you believe God, He makes that which may seem impossible to you, possible.

Faith

Psalm 46:10 (KJV)

*Be still, and know that
I am God: I will be
exalted among the
heathen, I will be
exalted in the earth.*

When you are still
God can move. Be
still so you can see the
mighty hand of God
move on your behalf.

Day
26

Faith

If you do not walk by
faith and your faith is
not ever tested, how
can you be trusted by
God?

Faith

Romans 4:20-21
(KJV)

He staggered not at the promise of God through unbelief; but was strong in faith, giving glory to God; And being fully persuaded that, what he had promised, he was able also to perform.

You must be fully persuaded that God will always do what he has said. Walk-in confidence knowing God cannot lie. He is the God of truth.

Faith

Numbers 23:19-20
(NIV)

God is not human, that he should lie, not a human being, that he should change his mind. Does he speak and then not act? Does he promise and not fulfill? I have received a command to bless; he has blessed, and I cannot change it.

God cannot change in any way, shape, or form. Therefore, if He said it, He makes it good. God has spoken, and God will fulfill.

Faith

Jeremiah 29:13
(KJV)

*And ye shall seek me,
and find me, when ye
shall search for me with
all your heart.*

Searching for God is
the matter of the
heart – Allow God to
restore you one beat
at a time. The heart
is a place where God
exists, so guard your
heart.

Faith

Ephesians 6:14 (KJV)

Stand therefore, having your loins girt about with truth, and having on the breastplate of righteousness.

What do you do when you have run out of options? S.T.A.N.D.

Seeking Truth And New Direction

Faith

I Samuel 30:8 (KJV)

*And David enquired at the
LORD, saying, Shall I pursue
after this troop? shall I overtake
them? And he answered him,
Pursue: for thou shalt surely
overtake them, and without fail
recover all.*

Go after what is in
your heart. Have faith
to believe what God
put in your heart to
pursue.

I John 4:19 (KJV)

We love him, because he first loved us.

You shall be recognized by love. Love is the most powerful evidence of being "born again" as a child of God. Genuine love comes from God.

Love

John 13:34-35 (ESV)

-

*A new commandment I give to
you, that you love one another:
just as I have loved you, you also
are to love one another. By this
all people will know that you are
my disciples, if you have love for
one another.*

Always be willing to
demonstrate the love
of God no matter
what. God is love,
wherever love is the
presence of God is
there.

**I Corinthians 13:13
(NLT)**

*Three things will last for-
ever—faith, hope, and
love—and the greatest of
these is love.*

Embrace the gift of
love. Love is the cen-
ter of our existence.
You can have faith,
you can have hope,
but without love, you
gain nothing.

Romans 5:8 (KJV)

*But God commendeth his
love toward us, in that,
while we were yet sinners,
Christ died for us.*

God proved his love
by giving us the best
gift, his Son the Lord
Jesus Christ even
though we were not
deserving of his love.

Romans 12:9-10
(KJV)

Let love be without dissimulation.
Abhor that which is evil; cleave to
that which is good. Be kindly
affectioned one to another with
brotherly love; in honour
preferring one
another...

Real love is what real
love does. Your love
for Christ is an
overview of what real,
sincere love looks like.
Do not pretend to
show love.

Love

I Corinthians 16:14
(ESV)

*Let all that you do be
done in love.*

What's love got to do
with what you do?
EVERYTHING!

Love

God's love is
consistent and His
love does not
change
God's love will always
bring peace and
comfort
God's love is revealed
to us through Jesus
Christ
God's love is poured
into us through his
Holy Spirit
God's love compels
us to love one
another

Psalm 136:26 (KJV)

*O give thanks unto the
God of heaven: for his
mercy endureth forever.*

When you don't have
anyone else, you can
always rely on the love
of God. His love lifts
you above anything.

Love

Romans 8:37-39 (KJV)

Nay, in all these things we are more than conquerors through him that loved us. For I am persuaded, that neither death, nor life, nor angels, nor principalities, nor powers, nor things present, nor things to come, nor height, nor depth, nor any other creature, shall be able to separate us from the love of God, which is in Christ Jesus our Lord.

Let love keep you. Be confident in his love. Know this, you are kept by his love therefore, nothing will be able to pull you away from his love.

Day
41

John 15:12 (NIV)

*My command is this:
Love each other as I have
loved you.*

Abide in the love of
Christ by showing
love toward one
another.

I John 3:1 (KJV)

Behold, what manner of love the Father hath bestowed upon us, that we should be called the sons of God: therefore, the world knoweth us not, because it knew him not.

No love like the love of the Father. Because of his love, we become sons of God.

Jeremiah 31:3 (KJV)

The LORD hath

appeared of old unto me, saying,
Yea, I have loved thee with an
everlasting love: therefore, with
lovingkindness have I drawn thee.

The love of God is from everlasting to everlasting. We are drawn to Christ because of his love. All it took was one drop of the blood of Christ that allows us to experience the love of the Father.

I John 4:7-8 (KJV)

Beloved, let us love one another: for love is of God; and every one that loveth is born of God, and knoweth God. He that loveth not knoweth not God; for God is love.

Let the seed of love grow. The more you fall in love with God, the more you will expose his love.

John 15:13 (KJV)

Greater love hath no man than this, that a man lay down his life for his friends.

Embrace the gift of love. What a friend we have in Jesus. It was his love that brought us back into a relationship with the Father.

**Colossians 3:14
(NIV)**

*And over all these virtues
put on love, which binds
them all together in perfect
unity.*

Love breeds unity that
holds everything
together.

Love is the existence
of matters of the
heart. The heart is
where God exists.
Guard and protect
your heart. Do not let
anything cause your
heart to flatline
because of the
absence of love.

Proverbs 3:3-4 (NIV)

Let love and faithfulness never leave you; bind them around your neck, write them on the tablet of your heart. Then you will win favor and a good name in the sight of God and man.

Be consistent in demonstrating the love of God, because it is through love favor will find you with God and man.

Luke 6:35 (ESV)

But love your enemies, and do good, and lend, expecting nothing in return; and your reward will be great, and you will be sons of the Most High; for He Himself is kind to ungrateful and evil men.

Never let what others may do to you, always show love despite if they will not return the love.

**Proverbs 10:12
(NIV)**

*Hatred stirs up conflict, but
love covers over all wrongs.*

Hatred is the beginning
of a lack of
understanding. Do
not get caught in a
conflict
because of the absence
of love. Love will
allow you to overlook
ignorance.

L.O.V.E.

Love Overcomes
Virtual Everything

Love is best seen in
actions and is mostly
identified by what you
do.

Love

Ephesians 4:31-32 (KJV)

Let all bitterness, and wrath, and anger, and clamour, and evil speaking, be put away from you, with all malice: And be ye kind one to another, tenderhearted, forgiving one another, even as God for Christ's sake hath forgiven you.

Put away anything that will keep you from flowing in the God kind of love.

Love

John 14:15 (KJV)

If ye love me, keep my commandments.

It is a sin not to demonstrate the love of God in Christ Jesus.

SIN is Self-Inflicted Neglect.

I John 4:9-12 (KJV)

In this was manifested the love of God toward us, because that God sent his only begotten Son into the world, that we might live through him. Herein is love, not that we loved God, but that he loved us, and sent his Son to be the propitiation for our sins. Beloved, if God so loved us, we ought also to love one another. No man hath seen God at any time. If we love one another, God dwelleth in us, and his love is perfected in us.

Get your heart right to put love in action so that you will meet the expectations of the Lord Jesus Christ.

Love

Love is not based on religious acts or deeds. Your loving attitudes and behavior are to reflect God's love.

Mark 12:29-31 (KJV)

And Jesus answered him, the first of all the commandments is, Hear, O Israel; The Lord our God is one Lord: And thou shalt love the Lord thy God with all thy heart, and with all thy soul, and with all thy mind, and with all thy strength: this is the first commandment. And the second is like, namely this, Thou shalt love thy neighbor as thyself. There is none other commandment greater than these.

Jesus raised the bar on showing love. With this commandment, you will be able to love beyond human capacity.

Isaiah 54:10 (NIV)

Though the mountains be shaken and the hills be removed, yet my unfailing love for you will not be shaken nor my covenant of peace be removed," says the Lord, who has compassion on you.

Walk in the stability of God's love for you. His love for you is unshakeable.

I John 4:9 (KJV)

In this was manifested the love of God toward us, because that God sent his only begotten Son into the world, that we might live through him."

Love lifted me!
Love lifted me!
When nothing else
could help
Love lifted me!

Psalm 136:26 (ESV)

Give thanks to the God of heaven, for his steadfast love endures forever.

Just Let Love Show – Do not let the light of God's love in you grow dim.

Move Forward

Isaiah 43:19 (KJV)

Behold, I will do a new thing; now it shall spring forth; shall ye not know it? I will even make a way in the wilderness, and rivers in the desert.

Embrace this season where the new thing will spring forth. What God has for you which cannot be hidden, God will cause people to see it, talk about it, desire it, and glorify God for it.

Day
61

Move Forward

Philippians 3:13-14 (KJV)

Brethren, I count not myself to have apprehended: but this one thing I do, forgetting those things which are behind, and reaching forth unto those things which are before, I press toward the mark for the prize of the high calling of God in Christ Jesus.

Only look back to see how far you have come. In the moments when you feel like giving up, press your way through. There is strength in your press.

Day

62

Move Forward

Romans 8:28 (KJV)

And we know that all things work together for good to them that love God, to them who are called according to his purpose.

Let God turn a bad situation into a good one, things always work out for your good.

Move Forward

Psalm 32:8 (ESV)

I will instruct you and show you the way to go; with My eye on you, I will give counsel.

The Lord is watching your every move. Seek the Lord for direction and guidance.

Move Forward

Psalm 119:105 (KJV)

*Thy word is a lamp unto
my feet and a light unto
my path.*

The Word of God
gives you light to
move forward on the
right path.

Move Forward

Proverbs 4:25-26
KJV

Let thine eyes look right on, and let thine eyelids look straight before thee. Ponder the path of thy feet, and let all thy ways be established.

You have been given your marching orders, move forward. No need to remain where you are. Greater can only come as you move forward.

Move Forward

Philippians 4:8 (KJV)

Finally, brethren, whatsoever things are true, whatsoever things are honest, whatsoever things are just, whatsoever things are pure, whatsoever things are lovely, whatsoever things are of good report; if there be any virtue, and if there be any praise, think on these things.

Stop being reactive on things that have no significance to your moving forward and become proactive with having a clear mindset to think on things that will bring forth a good report.

Move Forward

Psalm 37:23 (KJV)

*The steps of a good man
are ordered by the
LORD: and he
delighteth in his way.*

Ask God for guidance
in everything. Know
this, God cannot
guide your foot-
steps if you are not
willing to move your
feet.

Day

68

Move Forward

Acts 16:6-12 (KJV)

Now when they had gone

*throughout Phrygia and the region
of Galatia, and were forbidden
of the Holy Ghost to preach the
word in Asia, After they were
come to Mysia, they assayed to go
into
Bithynia: but the Spirit
suffered them not....*

God will close doors
when it is time to move
forward.
Because He knows you
will not move
unless your
circumstances f o r c e
y o u.

Move Forward

Exodus 14:13-14
(KJV)

*And Moses said unto the people,
Fear ye not, stand still, and see
the salvation of the LORD,
which he will shew to you today:
for the Egyptians whom ye have
seen today, ye shall see them again
no more forever. The LORD
shall fight for you, and ye shall
hold your peace.*

The only way you will
be able to see God
move on your behalf
is if you standstill.
Let the hand of the
Lord move you
forward.

Move Forward

Philippians 3:13 (KJV)
Matthew 19:26 (KJV)

Faith Forward –
Move beyond your limited capability

Accept No Limitations –
It is time to know what's real and what is not.

Except No Limitations –
If you expect more, God release more.

Embrace Definite Possibilities –
There is nothing too hard for God. When you see the spirit of God move, you move.

Move Forward

Hebrews 4:16 (KJV)

Let us therefore come boldly unto the throne of grace, that we may obtain mercy, and find grace to help in time of need.

God has given you access to His throne. You can co-labor with God as it creates an atmosphere to hear and the ability to see movement for advancement.

Move Forward

Isaiah 41:10 (ESV)

So do not fear, for I am with you; do not be dismayed, for I am your God. I will strengthen you and help you; I will uphold you with my righteous right hand.

Always remember that you never have to be in fear of your situation. Even when you don't understand, the Lord is your strength and help.

Move Forward

Jude 1:24-25 (KJV)

Now unto him that is able to keep you from falling, and to present you faultless before the presence of his glory with exceeding joy, To the only wise God our Saviour, be glory and majesty, dominion and power, both now and ever. Amen.

God will always help you as long as you put forth an effort. Do not fall by not doing your part to stay up.

Move Forward

Revelation 19:6 (KJV)
Revelation 21:6 (KJV)
Revelation 22:13 (KJV)

God is ALL!

Omnipotence means God is all-powerful – There is nothing that God cannot do for you. His power is infinite, or limitless.

Omniscience means God is all-knowing. – Nothing can be hidden from God. He knows the past, the present, and the future.

Omnipresence means God is all-present. – God is capable of being everywhere at the same time.

There is no god like the Almighty God. Who wouldn't want to serve a God who is OMNI! No one can duplicate His power.

No one can outwit him in wisdom. And, no one can take his place.

Move Forward

Romans 8:1 (KJV)

There is therefore now no condemnation to them which are in Christ Jesus, who walk not after the flesh, but after the Spirit.

Free at last! Living the Spirit-filled life. Knowing that Sin cannot control, condemn, or claim you!

Day

76

Move Forward

Isaiah 40:31 (KJV)

But they that wait upon the LORD shall re-new their strength; they shall mount up with wings as eagles; they shall run, and not be wea-ry; and they shall walk, and not faint.

Waiting on the Lord entails patient faith and is rewarded by His strength. In your weakness, He Strengthens you to soar above with whatever circumstances you may be faced with.

Day
77

Move Forward

Psalm 118:23 (KJV)

This is the LORD'S doing; it is marvelous in our eyes.

Get God involved in all of your situations. When God is in it things have to turn around.

Day
78

Move Forward

Psalm 34:8 (KJV)

O taste and see that the LORD is good: blessed is the man that trusteth in him.

This is the best time to try and experience just how good God is. Imagine the amount of joy you have just because you know Him.

Move Forward

Matthew 4:4 (KJV)

But he answered and said, It is written, Man shall not live by bread alone, but by every word that proceedeth out of the mouth of God.

Be willing to leave a deserted place which may cause hunger and fall in love with the word of God so you will be filled.

Move Forward

Galatians 5:22-23 (KJV)

But the fruit of the Spirit is love, joy, peace, longsuffering, kindness, goodness, faithfulness, gentleness, self-control. Against such there is no law.

Your character is identified by the fruit you bear.

Move Forward

It is time to S.H.I.F.T

—

Surrender to Him in
Faith for Tomorrow.
Shift your way of
thinking by walking in
faith toward your
future.

Move Forward

Psalm 43:4 (KJV)

Then will I go unto the altar of God, unto God my exceeding joy: yea, upon the harp will I praise thee, O God my God.

Begin to build an altar in your times of prayer. Find a place where it is just you and the Lord. Let it be a place of sacrifice so that it will bring you great joy.

Move Forward

Isaiah 1:19 (KJV)

If ye be willing and obedient, ye shall eat the good of the land:

Commit your ways to the Lord and be willing to do exactly what He says to do. Your obedience will release a fresh impartation of the blessings of God.

Move Forward

Micah 2:13 (ISV)

*God will stand up and
breakthrough in their presence.
Then they will pass through the
gate, going out by it. Their king
will pass in front of them with
the LORD at their head.*

Call the Breaker. Let
today be a day that
you call on the Lord,
who will lead you into
victory. Let the Lord
break down walls of
resistance and open a
gate for you today

Move Forward

Acts 16:26 (KJV)

And suddenly there was a great earthquake, so that the foundations of the prison were shaken: and immediately all the doors were opened, and every one's bands were loosed.

Know this, it is in the moment you think there is no solution, that is when you look to the Lord who knows no boundaries or limits. Allow God to reveal His power more extraordinarily. Call forth a sudden intervention.

Move Forward

I Thessalonians 3:11 (KJV)

*Now God himself and our
Father, and our Lord
Jesus Christ, direct our way unto
you.*

In the areas where
you feel as though
you have lost your
way, God will help
you get relocated and
on the right again.
He will give you new
strategies so you can
experience a new
sensation of divine
direction in all you
do.

Move Forward

Isaiah 43:21 (KJV)

This people have I formed for myself; they shall shew forth my praise.

There is a sound of transformation. Begin to watch what the Lord is doing globally. For there is a transformation taking place in your life. There will be new signs and news sounds, fresh revelation, and vision.

Move Forward

Romans 9:17 (NIV)

For Scripture says to Pharaoh: "I raised you up for this very purpose, that I might display my power in you and that my name might be proclaimed in all the earth."

God has not called you to blend in but to stand out. You have been born to be radical for God.

Move Forward

Do not be shaken by the obstacles before you, neither look at the mountain that stands in your way. In a blink of an eye, the Lord is against every obstacle and they will be consumed

Moave Forward

. Luke 10:19 (KJV)

Behold, I give unto you power to tread on serpents and scorpions, and over all the power of the enemy: and nothing shall by any means hurt you.

It is for you not to believe anything whatsoever has the power to harm you, for it is time to expect nothing other than every demonic power to be under your feet.

Day

91

Move Forward

John 9:25 (KJV)

He answered and said, whether he be a sinner or no, I know not: one thing I know, that, whereas I was blind, now I see.

God wants to open your eyes now to perceive things about your destiny and the future he has prepared for you. You have been given new eyes to see. Embrace this season of sharper vision.

Hope

Embracing the New: Do not stay limited only to what you have learned this far. Let go of old habits that you should not consider any longer. Be open to change. Out with the old and in with the new

Hope

Romans 4:21 (KJV)

And being fully persuaded that, what he had promised, he was able also to perform.

Be fully persuaded in expectation for a miracle. Don't look to the left or the right and wonder if it will ever come to pass. Look beyond logical circumstances and receive your miracle today.

Day
94

Hope

Psalm 107:29 (KJV)

He maketh the storm a calm, so that the waves thereof are still.

For though there are things that would add excess pressure, there is a place in the throne room of God where tensions can be dealt with. This is the time to be stress-free.

Hope

Isaiah 55:11 (ESV)

So shall my word be that goes out from my mouth; it shall not return to me empty, but it shall accomplish that which I purpose, and shall succeed in the thing for which I sent it.

You must proclaim the word of God. Apply the word to every situation. Whatever is spoken by God through His word will always manifest and come to pass. Get caught by the word of the Lord.

Hope

II Timothy 3:16-17 (KJV)

All scripture is given by inspiration of God, and is profitable for doctrine, for reproof, for correction, for instruction in righteousness: That the man of God may be perfect, thoroughly furnished unto all good works.

In this life, we have the answers we need, but we often look in the wrong places for the answers that are before us. Realize that the answers you seek are given to us by God in His word.

Hope

Psalm 119:11 (KJV)

Thy word have I hid in mine heart, that I might not sin against thee.

With the precious gift of the word of God, you will be able to overcome any sin and temptation that you may be faced with. Cherish the gift of God's word.

Day

98

Hope

Hebrews 4:12 (KJV)

For the word of God is quick, and powerful, and sharper than any two-edged sword, piercing even to the dividing asunder of soul and spirit, and of the joints and marrow, and is a discerner of the thoughts and intents of the heart.

The word of God has the power to reveal to you the true motive of your heart.

Day
99

Hope

Luke 11:28 (KJV)

But he said, yea rather, blessed are they that hear the word of God, and keep it.

Hearing the word of God is like taking it at face value. Be captivated by the word of God.

Day
100

Hope

Psalms 119:71 (KJV)
John 10:10 (KJV)
Romans 15:13 (KJV)

Allow this season to
be a season of
empowerment. I
want to encourage you
to be empowered and
apply the following;

Learn from the past.
Celebrate and live in
the present.

Work toward and
hope for the future.

Hope

II Corinthians 1:20 (KJV)

For all the promises of God in him are yea, and in him Amen, unto the glory of God by us.

Always be willing to flow in the weight of the promises of God. He always makes good on them.

Hope

Psalm 43:4 (NIV)

Then I will go to the altar of God, to God, my joy and my delight. I will praise you with the lyre, O God, my God.

Create an altar of sacrifice and give yourself to God. It is at the altar that the Lord God will grant your every request.

Hope

Even as you look and
experience some
challenges begin to
say, It Is Well! When
it would be easy to
draw attention to
difficulty and despair,
say it is well! Know
that each time you say,
it is well, you open the
way to the miraculous
and the new life shall
enter your soul.

Hope

Psalm 118:23 (KJV)

This is the LORD's doing; it is marvelous in our eyes.

It is awesome to know that the Lord will do wonderful things for you. Thank him that you don't have to worry about how things will turn out because he is already doing some marvelous things that are amazing in our sight.

Hope

Mark 6:50 (KJV)

For they all saw him, and were troubled. And immediately he talked with them, and saith unto them, be of good cheer: it is I; be not afraid.

Do not be afraid of any situation that you may see with your natural eye. Be encouraged in knowing God is with you in the midst of it all.

Hope

The Lord
Remembers You

–

Never assume that
what seems to be a
barren season will not
change in one
moment. The Lord
will listen intently to
your prayers. And
because He
remembers you,
whatever you ask in
prayer, it will come to
pass and you will see
the fruit of it.

Hope

Hebrews 10:23
(NIV)

*Let us hold unswervingly
to the hope we profess, for
he who promised is
faithful.*

Hope is knowing that
no matter what the
circumstance, God
makes a promise to
help us to overcome.
Hold on to the hope
that is within you.
God is faithful.

Hope

Philippians 1:6
(KJV)

*Being confident of this very thing,
that he which hath begun a good
work in you will perform it until
the day of Jesus Christ:*

God never starts anything that He cannot complete. When God begins a work in us, He will see it through to completion. Let him continue the work he started.

Hope

Psalm 33:18 (ESV)

*Behold, the eye of
the LORD is on those who
fear him,
on those who hope in his
steadfast love.*

The eye of God is
upon you to watch
over your every move.

Hope

Psalm 39:7 (NLT)

*And so, Lord, where do I
put my hope? My only
hope is in you.*

Your hope in God will
always lead you
through times of
struggle.

Day
111

Hope

Shake off what was in
order to become what
is. Do not let any
distractions keep you
from moving forward
in hope of a better
you.

Hope

Romans 1:18 (NIV)

I pray that the eyes of your heart may be enlightened in order that you may know the hope to which he has called you, the riches of his glorious inheritance in his holy people.

It is important to know how much you are worth to God. Knowing the power of God will increase the worth of your relationship with Him.

Hope

Psalm 139:14 (KJV)

*I will praise thee; for I
am fearful-
ly and wonderfully made:
marvelous are thy works;
and that my soul knoweth
right well.*

You have been called.

—

You have been
justified.

—

You have been
glorified in Christ.

Hope

Put the word of God
in every situation.
Because your future
will be happier than
your past was sad.

Hope

Hebrews 12:2 (KJV)

*Looking unto Jesus the
author and finisher
of our faith; who for the
joy that was set before him
endured the cross,
despising the shame, and
is set down at the right
hand of the throne of
God.*

Allow the Lord
access to bring
sudden intervention
in everything you go
through. Because
he endured, you can
too.

Day
116

Hope

Whatever you go
through, the hope in
knowing IT was not
designed to take you
out but to set you up.
Know that IT is
finished.
Walk in the power
over your IT.
Rise above your IT.
Let go of your IT.

Hope

You never have to justify your past by reducing the value of who you are now. Your value is far greater than any label that you or anyone else may have put on you.

Hope

Isaiah 1:19 (KJV)

If ye be willing and obedient, ye shall eat the good of the land.

Get ready to walk with E.B.T .
Enjoying my Blessed Transformation.

Hope

The issue is already
settled. The miracle is
what you have in your
house.

Hope

Jude 1:24-25 (KJV)

Now unto him that is able to keep you from falling, and to present you faultless before the presence of his glory with exceeding joy, to the only wise God our Savior, be glory and majesty, dominion and power, both now and ever. Amen.

ABOUT THE AUTHOR

Dr. David R. Watkins is the Overseer by the unction of the Holy Spirit of Redeemer's Purpose Ministries, Inc. R.P.M.I. has been birthed through Dr. Watkins by God. Dr. Watkins is a native of Tampa and grew up to be what God has predestined him to be. He accepted the Lord at a very young age and has always wanted to seek and please God. He has a great love for God and the people of God. Called by God, Dr. Watkins has been ministering the Word of God since the age of 17 years old. He accepted the call and was ordained as a minister of the gospel. He is the husband of Lady Tonya Watkins and the Father of five children, Shayla, Christa, Terence, Jerod, a daughter in love Jayla, and a granddaughter Janiya who are all dear to his heart. He is definitely a family man. He gives honor to his mother, Evelyn Streets, who has been an inspiration in his life

Dr. Watkins wanted to learn more about God; therefore, as the Lord began to crown him with wisdom, his desire grew even more for the things of God.

Dr. Watkins was raised as an Episcopalian and served as an Acolyte assistant to the Priest. Later his mother began attending Pentecostal and

Holiness churches, where he found a greater zeal for God. He then began attending Bethany Missionary Baptist Church, where he was baptized. There he served as an usher, van transporter, and later became a deacon after receiving the baptism of the Holy Spirit.

Dr. Watkins has helped to establish transitional homes and has worked with Abe Brown Ministries Ready4Work. Dr. Watkins has labored and served as an Assistant Pastor, a Pastor, a Teacher, and an Overseer for several churches to include: Agapao Christian Fellowship Church, Covenant Missionary Baptist Church, to name a few. He even served as a Headmaster for Harvest Christian Academy and has helped establish several other churches and Christian schools.

After prayer and confirmation, Dr. Watkins has received and accepted the call into the office of the Apostle. He was consecrated to the office of an Apostle in March 2012 by his spiritual Father and Apostle, Apostle Dr. J.L. Cash Sr. of Kingdom Workers International, Inc. Apostle Watkins has a great heart for the homeless and less fortunate. He is working diligently in establishing a homeless shelter that will house, feed, and clothe homeless veterans and anyone else who is homeless. The Redeemer's Purpose Village of Hope will shelter the homeless and less fortunate and provide job training, placements, education, and restoration spiritually, physically, and emotionally. Redeem the whole person. Apostle Watkins is the owner and founder of Sha'Rista Catering Company and plans to open Sha'Rista Family Restaurant. He has been in the catering business since the age of 12years old and has a great love for bringing couples wedding dreams into a blessed reality.

Dr. Watkins has a host of churches and is a spiritual mentor to pastors and leaders in several states and globally, including Nigeria, Africa, and others. He desires to go worldwide and preach and teach God's Word to all wounded that require restoration. The Spirit of the Lord has placed in Dr. Watkins's heart to begin to do mission work over in Africa, and many other countries as the Spirit of God leads. God has prepared him for a great work, according to Isaiah 40:31.

In addition to all of this, Dr. Watkins labors by the unction of the Spirit of the Lord in the ministry he established in 2008, Restoration Worldwide

Ministries, later renamed Redeemer's Purpose Ministries Inc.

The mission of Redeemers Purpose Ministries, Inc. is to:

1. Be the ministry that fulfills the great commission of the Lord Jesus Christ. (Matthew 28:18-20). His passion is to continue to move forward in doing the Father's business through the Lord Jesus Christ.

2. Maintain spiritual worship by preaching and teaching God's Word and strengthening and edifying one another in faith. To be the ministry that demonstrates love and walks in love. (I Corinthians Chapter 13).

3. Make an impact in our local community, our nation, and even worldwide.

4. Be the ministry that walks in obedience to God and his word and fulfills the purpose and the plan of God.

Finally, Apostle Watkins has been elected as Chaplin for O.C.M. (One Community & More, Dallas, Texas). He is also a member of W.L.M.I. Apostolic Council and is a Certified Life Coach that brings revelation, insight, impartation, and inspiration to all seeking growth and development.

Stay Tuned for additional publications scribed through this mighty vessel; to God, be all the glory!

Connect with Apostle, Dr. David R. Watkins

On Facebook @ david.watkins.39

Facebook @ RedeemersPM

Email: Redeemerspm@outlook.com

Email: DavidRWatkinsBooks@gmail.com

Web: Www.RedeemersPurpose.com

www.ingramcontent.com/pod-product-compliance
Lightning Source LLC
Chambersburg PA
CBHW060328050426
42449CB00011B/2697